Praise for
Midwestern Poet's Incomplete Guide to Symbolism

In *Midwestern Poet's Incomplete Guide to Symbolism*, Erica Anderson-Senter's candid, sensual voice invites us through fields of grief, loss, desire, and myth. "Why couldn't we have loved harder in this universe, / more robustly?" the speaker asks. Anderson-Senter bends the laws of physics to imagine different universes, ones in which the dead father is a "white gull, the sea in [his] body." Although we inhabit other universes, these poems root us deep in Midwestern landscapes as we encounter litanies, psalms, and a lush, unsentimental tenderness that sings out "that swift, / startling joy" in the same breath as gutting loss. This is an extraordinary, courageous debut collection.

— EMILY MOHN-SLATE, author of *The Falls*

In Erica Anderson-Senter's debut full-length collection, *Midwestern Poet's Incomplete Guide to Symbolism*, we hear a poet making breathtaking sense of the most unbearable pain in her life—the death of her father, her marriage, her unborn child. The lines in this book are vespers, a prayer to the broken hearted. We are swept up in the beauty of form, the spaces in between, the images of a red-tail hawk, and a cantering horse. The book masterfully hones the sounds of grief, guttural and raw, flowing through a body, a mouth, a soul. She writes, "I am a fern growing, dirt deep in my blood," and so are we.

— SARAH SANDMAN, author of *I Speak Moan* and *The Sinew of 47 Years*

Out of grief, out of longing, out of her ravishing gift for noticing, comes this numinous and memorable debut by Erica Anderson-Senter, whose sensibility has been born out of her gifts for surviving. As the title tells us, this is a Midwestern book, but what do we mean by that? Here it means the settings and the vernacular music are tuned to a particular place, with its creatures and soil and people whose lives are at the center of the country, if not the country's larger consciousness. I adore the rough music of this book, its candid appraisals, and this poet's fearless descriptions of the sources of fear, sadness, love, life.

— MARK WUNDERLICH, author of *God of Nothingness* and *The Earth Avails*

MIDWESTERN POET'S
INCOMPLETE GUIDE TO SYMBOLISM

Erica Anderson-Senter

Rochester, Massachusetts
www.EastOverPress.com

Midwestern Poet's Incomplete Guide to Symbolism

Erica Anderson-Senter

ISBN 978-1-958094-13-6

BOOK DESIGN: EK LARKEN

COVER DESIGN: Spock and Associates
Cover images are from *The Compendium of Illustrations* (Agile Rabbit Editions 2006), published by The Pepin Press, www.pepinpress.com

EastOver Press encourages the use of our publications in educational settings. For questions about educational discounts, contact us online:. www.EastOverPress.com *or* info@EastOverPress.com

PUBLISHED IN THE UNITED STATES OF AMERICA BY

EASTOVER
— P R E S S —

Rochester, Massachusetts
www.eastoverpress.com

for all the men who've died in my life,
even those still living

CONTENTS

Creation Poem for Lovers

In the beginning two souls—
        no—
In the beginning you & me—
        no—
In the beginning two suns spread
        across darkness—
        yes—

In the beginning the first Eucharist
        was not body & blood—
        no—the first Eucharist
        was body & blood & heat
        between two suns whispering
        genesis, invention, handiwork, *thing*
        lips to lips, in the skies.
        Yes—

In the beginning there was not one god
        but the promise of holy &
        baby, you & I are holy:

        October fog on cornstalks in purple dawn,
        when you fall asleep & your breathing shifts,
        the small creek we consider,
            tiny silver fish jerking their slick bodies,
        when we, in golden light of evening, fight
        in the parking lot.

We created harvest & purple & sleep & evening &
street lights & all the veiny streams coursing
through the land of our bodies—

        yes—we did that in the beginning.

Autobiography: Summers at My Babysitter's House

When I was a child,
wild with sap, I ran with boys
before the seam of my legs
meant sex. Feral toes torn,

bare-feet, green stained and leather.
These, my legs; these, my feet only meant:
to run, to stand, to bend beneath
the basketball hoop. My blood, fat

with purple blackberries vultured
by my own slight hands, shoved
in my moon-mouth. I collected
tangles in my corn-silk hair.

I, the native daughter of Indiana
evenings, licked clean by Ursa Major.
Here, I learned to run, to hide, to bend
beneath the weight of men.

Writing about Birds on the Anniversary of Your Death
for dad

Someone said, once, a robin held silent vigil next to her feather-
bare baby on a busy road. Stood dumb-shocked near the dead

hatchling, knocked from the nest with no wings to catch wind.
Dull-eyed, feathered thing standing still, not moving

for cars, not moving—tell me she's too dim-witted to feel,
suddenly, loss; to suddenly lose and know it. Tell me she

can't know it. Tell me there's still hollow hope that one living
thing can dodge heart-hurt of quick, cruel dying.

Don't let the dense bird know it. Because if she can
because if *she* can
                    if   she   can,

                              what does   that   mean for me.

First

The afternoon a pink spot blossomed
on my cotton panties for the very first time
I thought I had cut myself, somehow a ruckus
while exploring my own flesh. I would slide my
hands between my legs in the shower,
feel the shudder of an unexplained—

No. This slight alert of womanhood came softly.

I first bled at my grandmother's house.
That day how could I know that blood
would soak through my denim in eighth grade?
I am sorry this happened. I am even more sorry
this happened in art class, forcing me to ask
Matt Foy for his sweatshirt: a savior, the boy
with curly hair. The blood would come unannounced,
singing it's siren song of estrogen as I walked
with *Lord of the Flies* pressed to my chest.

Years after, I had a lover entice me to his bed
while I was bleeding. Then I left him
because another man asked me to dinner.
I am sorry to have ruined his sheets.
That night we slept, windows
open, in blood and sweat. Understand,
this was no covenant. Instead a propulsion
of lust.

My grandmother came into the dark bathroom
on that August afternoon and celebrated
this small strawberry stain with an embrace,
a waterfall of women before her—
praising this streak of blood.

Two Deaths, One Poem

Late one autumn, if not five, probably ten years ago
hiking a trail with my husband we
come upon a decomposing deer.
The fur of this creature, loose off the bone, blonder
than it should be caught wind and blew away.
The mandible of this beast graying in the mud—
back molars worn into small troughs—I ask him,
   Can I touch the thing?
We walk near, lean down, and consider the lifeless
thing. I say, the leg of a dead deer is still an impressive
thing. What I mean here is:
the decomposition starts slowly—we don't know we
are coming apart.
It starts with a girl's soft middle—she might say,
   Here, your hand here and then he might say
   No.
Step by step they find themselves next to a dead
deer in a meadowed field near a river
without one recollection of what kind of wild
they once were. What I want to say is:
a divorce doesn't happen in a day,
the death starts at dusk, two
beasts baying at a moon, lamenting.

Blue Stars Due North

It is summer 2000 when I watch the body
of my childhood home burn around 3 am.

You died that night.
But splintered from this life, maybe another

exists where, instead of ashes, your bones
are blue stars due north. Your nose

a wild strawberry growing near a mossy-
barn—pink, pleasantly round.

I am calm in this other life and you
are a speckled trout, a line of green

on your fishbody. I don't think of drowning,
I don't envision your teeth gray

from smoke-slathered screams. I am
my own palm outstretched in this other life—

this other life you are a porch swing—
you are a small candle in a winter night,

you are another man, not my father,
but a window washer named Frank.

You are a white gull, the sea in your body, and
I am a fern growing, dirt deep in my blood.

How a Horse Thinks

It isn't all grass and canter and tail swish immediacy.
It isn't always field unfurled and naked horizon
    or moon-backed prairie.
Observant to anointed grassland,
it isn't just about anointed grassland.
It isn't hoofbeat, dirtdusty knees, and unswept barrel.
It isn't only holy tongues unheard
    or lungs in, lungs out, sweat, and privilege of strength.
It isn't tunnel vision and firespook busting through
    rivers up to throat-latch.
It isn't grief—it isn't gallop and gait and interrupted stripe,
it isn't the beast-fur carrying burden and broken bosom
    into weeds.
Horse hearts are heavy with a sense of divine,
rearing and breaking with weight:
    the dead, *this* dead, this *one* dead.

How Many Hours?

We once drove through Texas pointing out clouds
and birds and bluebonnets and license plates and sometimes

we sat in silence, in the Volkswagen. I remember the first scissor-
tailed fly catcher—she was sitting on a wire fence. Sometimes

I'll remember leaving Oklahoma and rejoicing in the Texan
terrain. I was born there, in that state, and sometimes

I think of moving there, now. Sell my shit and tumble
my ass south. Be a small thing in a big state. Sometimes

I miss you. Mostly, I don't. That trip opened us up
to each other. You: vast sky. Me: long, gray road. Sometimes

I miss the promise. We drove for hours—Indiana to Nevada,
but I remember Texas the most. It's been 4 years. Sometimes

that ball of time feels fake. I count the years on my fingers
before I fall asleep. Sometimes.   Only sometimes.

Handbook for the Almost Divorced

Stand in front of the mirror.
Use your index finger to lift
your left breast; let it fall.
Checking for elasticity, do it again.
Index all the adjectives he uses to describe you.
Pluck the one that seems most false,
use it back in a complete sentence.
Fake left, pass right.
Stock up on compliments
from strangers in pea-coats, boys at the bar,
local performers, that one old lady
at the post office, baristas with blonde hair,
Tennessee women who coo *yes, yes, you—*
ration   them   carefully;
cans of beans in the apocalypse.
Where did it all start, this trouble?
Ask this endlessly.
Trace the origins of certain demise
like bloodlines; as old as Ellis Island.
Resist the temptation to fall to your knees
and beg his forgiveness.
Or do.
Do fall down
and moan.

Lifecycle of a Father

A man is first a boy, and before that,
he is one small-petaled blossom attached to the arms
of his mother and before that, even, a man is all sweat
and riverwater and impossible electricity and
another man moving a woman's legs apart.

A man is, at last, one final breath,
a gulp of impossible air before his lungs
completely deflate. He then, in the beginning
of one summer, is buried under grass and soil
and the dust from a country road in LaPorte County.

I always know I'm close; the sign that says
"Lamb's Chapel" rests two left turns
before the cemetery. I counted the roads
with riverstones in my pocket—
little trinkets for his headstone,
in case he needs to remember movement.

Breaking Up on the Moon

We are weighed down with the want of each other
exactly 16 percent less here. I swallow teaspoons
of gravity while we are here. Starlings suspended
above our heads, faintly out of reach. Atmosphere
out of reach. *Who brought birds to the moon*, I ask?
The lines of my body, blurring against the bare sky,
quietly come apart: soft fat of my thigh, slope of my heel,
curve of my calf press against the hollow hallway of black.
I can't remember how we got here. Did we bring those birds?
Rolling our failed intentions between our fingertips
we are polite with one another, saying,
You have dust on your face, let me get that for you.

Permission
to Mary Oliver

The white moths of morning
slide out from between the pink
lobes of my lungs—I breathe
in my quiet house.

Yes, Mary, I try to move through
this space, this life the way
you might. I grant permission
to my legs—move me to the riverbed.
To my feet—dig into the mud.
To my hands—pick up every stone
and marvel.

A Small Parable about a Father

My father was born blond in late December.
Just a few years later, let's say sixteen, still blond,
stupidly beautiful, he discovered whiskey, the tawny
skin of a tender lover—
he never had a chance, really. From his turmoil
every single country ballad balled up and fell
from his broad back.
How many ways can a man die
before he dies on a June night?
Listen. What I'm saying here is:
my father died drunk, divorced, and alone,
in a housefire the summer I turned sixteen.
And if that doesn't come straight from the mountain
of despair—
what exactly does?

Slatted, Divided, Separated

Here, we don't acknowledge the dead.
The nuthatch scurries the tree,
cocks her head only for food.
Here, I sit at my desk,
red wine to my right, blood rich teeth
stained purple. Here, I say: *sex in the morning*,
and *life like leaves*, and *tremble* and *sway*.
Here, race horses live, splintered bones
and foam-saddled sweat. Here, we will not separate
death and gods and tender muscles between ribs.
Here, the moon air throws spores.
The silver maple turns her back to the rain.
Here, the rain, the rain, the rain.
I, slatted and divided here, don't acknowledge the dead.

Heirloom

From my grandmother I learned firm
tomatoes ripen in the window on the sill
exposed to sunlight:

morning light to golden hour.
I used this in my marriage
every summer in a perfect kitchen

for sunlight. My husband hated
tomatoes. I never understood this
or, as I can now say, how we just let

this tender fruit between us rot.

In Praise of the Divorce: A Psalm

Oh, body, let the marigold center blossom in early evening;
we stretch far into the week with our sun-head, each new
November one long day.
Oh, how we used to rot under bags of trash,
but now, sweet body, we have unfastened our arms
to reach far into the clear pools to grasp,
forefinger and thumb, the smoothest pebbles.

Are we not worthy of tiny stones?

Let our soft belly hold the fruit, each tender pear
of the coming years, let us take each morning,
the sunrise on the tip of our tongue;
let us taste the pink skin of our new lover.
Oh, body, in praise of the west, trace
each branch on our palm—let us braid
hours and arms with seaweed and sycamore leaves.
Let us take, oh body, what we need and press our feet
into the mud and place smooth stones into our mouth.

Still Can Not

I press my ear against the belly of a black dog
named Cocoa, knotted with pups, nipples
prune-sized and pulled down to the gravel.
She is my babysitter's dog. Summer days here
smell milkweed and corn, taste blackberries
and sweat. I am small, she is kind to me—
sniffing my knees as I walk.
I rub her ears and purr about the babies
she is always about to mother.

Cocoa was not at my knees when the sunburst
of my scalp burnt red with each breath, sobbing
for the split black snake torn from Keith's slingshot.
Running, hiding the cellar kept quiet and held me
damp. My little pink fingers could not hold the slit
closed, could not keep insides from spilling
all over the dry grass, my purrs could not calm
the writhing, rolling body of that one black snake.

Still can not.

Lot's Wife Revisited

What exactly is a first fruit? If I don't
fake-kill my fake-son, am I even faithful?
I don't farm, but if I did and didn't offer
the fattest watermelon to a greedy god,
would he, instead, murder every melon
by poisoning the vine?
Who gives this god the power to make
us flinch so hard we break our teeth?

Between my legs, there's a small berry—
I have tended its growth. When I was very
young, Jehovah spoke for its juice.
How is this a thing? Some being
who uses the name Most High spoke
for the fruit of my body before I bled
the blood of womanhood.

What kind of father kills son
after son after son: water, cross,
stone, you name it. And pays no homage
to daughters. My ram is my own,
I will eat all the apples. How can
Ancient of Days take and take?
How many sacrifices before I crawl
out from under this profound guilt.

My Mother Likes to Say

We come from poor, so we know—
we come from potted meats and worn-
out panties, so when we stock up
for the pandemic, we buy shelf-stable milk.

We come from a line that lasts:
we fight on the playground, rusted
swing chains and gravel. We'll survive
this—your dad beat the shit out of me
so we'll survive this—

We come from poor. We don't slather
in wants, only step over our needs.
We make our own money, keep a clean house.
Poor doesn't mean dirty. We know how
to fry an egg, drive a stick.

We know how to escape. We know how
to hunker down and stay, rub dirt
on our faces. We hide from a drunk
husband in an old attic between two dressers.
If he finds us, he might become confused.

Last Note to My Neighbor

Slicing ginger as my knife allows and running water
over my hands, you are dead. Even though you were young.

Thinking about you near the toilet, bent in your last pain—
cats sniffing the crown of your head, maybe chewing

on your fingertips, lapping the blood from your ear.
My cat's head is warm, smells wild. I put my nose

between his ears. You are dead.
I didn't say anything to you last time I saw you out,

gave a meek wave while the wind moved your hair.
My floors are dirty with winter and your brother

cleans out your apartment. He doesn't seem sad.
I don't know him. I didn't know you—not really—

Once you told me about the hawk that lives
above our house. *It grabbed a sparrow* you said

right out of the air you said. *I looked up right in time
to feel a drop of blood on my forehead.* How lucky,

I thought. Marked, I thought. *I watched the feathers
float to the ground.*

The Bread Factory
for Andy

When it is snowing on quiet January nights, I think of our old apartment: when we were folding into the heavy darkness and wet snow as we walked to our favorite bar. We had a lot of *ours* in that small life—our bed, our sink, our black cat and his brother the tabby, our debt, our lamps and rugs—we moved through doorways with no idea that in a few short years, you would be my ex-lover and I, yours.

Ex—prefix of extract, extinct, extinguish. Jesus, where did we take the left turn that lead us to this specific spot? Me—on the other side of town and you still there on our green couch?

Do you remember those cold winters we'd walk to Henry's, our mouths wanting one gin for me, whiskey for you? Feeling like nothing could peel us apart, holding gloved hands while the Sunbeam factory filled the space between our bodies with the warm smell of baking bread—

Physics of a Daughter in Survival

In this universe, water is only water and does not dilute whiskey.
In another there are 116 ways to pet a dog; the way
he, in this one, kicks my small schnauzer does not appear.
Two universes over, housesfires consume wood, some metals,
cans of food, school photos, but never drunk dads.
Four universes under he teaches me, tiny-toothed, to fight
gravity, to ride a bike, to fall down and bleed. In our universe,
please, can he still be fishing for channel cats off the back of the boat?
In the universe adjacent, he calls me to check,
     hey, how much salt in that one chicken recipe?
Why couldn't we have loved harder in this universe,
more robustly?

     Why can't I forgive; let the red maple burn then drop its leaves?

When I Am Dead

Feed my poems to wild dogs. Be careful, though, they are wild dogs. They'll eat anything, even your hands. Find willing strangers and tell them the story about my mom—No, not the one you're thinking. The one where we, she and I, big and little, same skin, pull off Hwy 32 with apples and carrots and flat-palms to fatten-up someone else's horse. That light-bay knew us by smell, knew us by noise. This is the kindness I take.

Bury my body, dumb tongue of a thing, in hard earth. Say something cliché: *because life was never easy, never soft.* Drop the dirt terrible. When I am dead cut your hair on the summer solstice, walk backward around our favorite bar, memorize names of full moons: strawberry, you'll say, hunter's, wolf, flower, sturgeon, buck. What does it all mean? What does it all mean? Say *this was her favorite food* after every meal in a real asshole way, like you knew. You didn't know. Remember the red poppies outside of Huntington, perched on that dirty hill, little licks of swaying Pentecost. The holy in this is heavy. When I am dead, please don't cry. Weep! I mean it, weep for me. Throw your body down and really make a show of it.

Or surrender me to the dark. Quiet, no fuss. It is where I've been walking all this time. All this time.

The One with an Ex, a Stray Cat, and Elves

It's Saturday—my cats are meowing
at a stray on my back stoop. A boy
in college said my eyes were gray,
like the longing for sea—he read
a lot of Tolkien, can't blame a guy
for trying to woo me with words
and elves. The stray pawing
at my screen is also gray and furious
at everyone but me. I've watched him
hiss and spit at a neighbor—
feral recognizes feral so I give him food.

Two years ago I left my husband.
Our growth dammed up by booze
and secrecy. What I mean is:
he was always drinking and I,
fucking other men. We thought,
at first, it was a forever-thing.
Turns out, 15 years is a little too long
for a wild-thing, even if there's kindness
and food at the doorstep.

Small Dance of Memory

You might stand under the disco ball,
confetti light on your cheek, as you
consider this June night—alone.
You will order one more before you
come home, the house is still standing
which means
your earth is still wet with opportunity,
a deep lake. You might see into the future,
it's dark, you might say, because you die
in two hours.
You do die in two hours—first,
you slow dance one more time, one last
beer, one more deep breath as you walk
outside to hitch a ride home
where your daughter sleeps downstairs.
You'll die in two hours which means,
I'm still here 21 years later
thinking of you standing under the disco ball,
the small light on your face, alone.

Early Morning Prayer
after James Wright

I close my eyes, and think of water.
Now, I am in my fifteen year old body: tight
and June-time tanned. You are here, too,
on this Tennessee lake—not dead—
Instead,
holding a channel cat by his bottom lip.
We, father and daughter, laugh with a joy
we can not name—it cuts through the wet morning.
Here, on this side, I am 37 in December.
How many lifetimes leak through our fingers?

Genesis

In the beginning somehow sound, somehow death, somehow sex,
somehow the lost sparrow of perfect song,
somehow a dissertation
on particular flight patterns in iamb—
> *you know,   I can't,   belong,   exist,*
> *implode,   destroy,*
somehow no anxiety, somehow only hazy woe.
Creation is regretful, it is disquiet
and somehow, in the beginning,
it never began.
We bump into each other in the dark.

Instructions on Joy

Look out your southfacing window,
           how many robins perched on middle wires?
Look under the pile of clothes on your bedroom floor.
Look inside each of your books, flip to page 16.
           Open each drawer in your small apartment and
Look.
Look under the snow near your mailbox,
           wait eight months, then look under the litter
           of leaves left by the elm.
Look at your palm's lifeline, that trench that splits
           into two fates, or two branches, or two curses.
Look at a stranger after she sneezes—*bless you*, you
           should say. If she doesn't hear you,
           bless her again.
           Tucked in with your sheets:
Look there, or in between your nephew's milk teeth.
Look up the phrase *bless you*,
           ask God to bestow favor,
           lollipops thrown at a small-town parade
           and please, save the wrath for another day.
Look in your lover's eyes right before the pale-moon
           sings and say three times:
           There's no place like home
           There's no place like home
           There's no place like home.
           He might become uneasy, but kiss him again
           to quell his unease.

Look, I don't really know the exact map—
           I do know how it tastes and that we're close.

Silhouettes of Birds Against the Evening Sky
after Shira Erlichman

I want to touch your elbow: *this way* I'll say as we both walk
into this used bookstore on a Saturday.

I want to touch your palm: different than holy pilgrim's kiss, but
still kind of the same.

I want to touch your shoulder: comfort is a far off friend and we
both know it.

I want to touch your lips: sing the words you first sang,
the creation of this thing between us. *This way*, you'll say,
stepping into the Thursday morning.

I want to touch your leg: climb the small hills, palm to palm
with oaks on the trail.

I want to touch your knee: small moment between us: you
in my bed, me in my bed, both reading in dim light.

I want to touch your ribs: brush them as I say *this way* and take off
your shirt.

I want to touch your finger: you point into the sky and I'll say blue
heron or egret or small wren outside of the clouds. We both eat
silhouettes of birds against the evening sky.

I want to touch your thigh: *listen*, I'll say, *hush, it's okay. I promise: I
know, I know, I know* as I shake my head, tenderly.

I want to touch your eyes: yellow pond-lily, my favorite beige
sweater, each word I write.

I want to touch your neck: warm blood flushes as my palms rest
on either side.

Life is a wreck but we both have this skin.

The People in This Poem Are Capable of Joy

A few years ago on my dead dad's birthday
I miscarried—bled my way through a double-shift
at a bar I hated. A few days before my therapist told me
that out of the worst circumstances, *good things can exist*,
she had her daughter alone. A few months later, my psychic
said my dad didn't want me to have *this* baby—
she also said that the world was mine—movement
was in my future. I do move. Everyday. With wind
and whimsy of life, simple happinesses like my lover's
thumbnail, the shrill call of a starling, how the man
in Picasso's painting has given up; yes, even surrender.
Even surrender makes me move. I don't have a baby.
I do have these legs that take me up and down stairs,
a small apartment with books, running water, a bed,
and a cat who curls next to me when I'm sad.
I have a yellow flower my neighbor left on my door-
step and a favorite pen. I have all these things—
and occasionally, waves of joy.

Every Small Thing

I want my bones to feel the weight
of my lover every gauzy morning.
I want his cheek in my palm, I want
every small thing to light up and point
to him, shit, I just want him.
I want to look out the window
and see starlings by the thousands
in the crabapple tree just so I can say:
you can't imagine how many blackbirds
I saw today—I want him to guess
how many then I'll say: *No. More.*
I want each phone call to pull
a golden wire stretched from the core
of the earth up through my body
and out my ear, because his voice
is physical, a heft and husk to it.
I want each small horse to eat
out of my palm—I want to tell
my lover that, yes, in fact, small horses
are born to gods. I want to feel
the birth of something this electric
in every single lifetime after this one
until all energy rests on his top lip
while he walks to his car.

A Love Poem Featuring a Bird

Moving my body from bed to bathroom,
from car to classroom, from desk to sink
takes a musclebone strength—
but walking behind my lover
on an April morning is different.
There is no real gravity, only a sirensong
rope from his body attached to mine—
keeping us tethered, grounded—
silver thread pulled from Saturn's
most delicate ring.
And, please hear me, I am completely
and sincerely worn out from writing about him
but even the callous on my finger is a sweet-
spot in this disappearing universe
where the only real thing that might matter
is when he turns toward me on that certain
April morning and points out a wren
flitting from one tree to another.

Pregnancy Litany, in Time of Surplus
in response to What to Expect When You're Expecting

God of two horses on a hill
    of plenty
    of appleseeds and small round blueberries;

God of naked limbs and flowering cabbage
    of sweet-meat avocados
    of the poet's fig and plum
    of multitudes and bounty and fertility;

God of Indiana muskmelon with bones,
    of pomegranate seeds and one precise cherry,

                growing.

God of tadpole genesis;
God of the enough;
God of each raspberry,

              plump with blood;

God of harvest soil and zenith;
God of fullness and filling and each mass that moves;
God of kitten paw and lamb skin;
God of the quiet butternut squash
    of skin that multiplies, wealth in lungs
    of tiny hairs that sway with river smell;

God of plethora and stores of smooth stones;
    of evening honeydew sweet with spit
    of sweat
    of abundance:

Hear me, please, and forgive.

Sparrows in the Goldenrod
wedding poem for Nate and Christie

Growing against the fence,
a feral goldenrod, wild with wind
and luster, moves.

The autumn morning pours the coffee
while summer slows to gone.
Palm-sized sparrows skim

the skin of this blue sky, weaving
between the boughs as if their
small bodies were created to flit

through in *this* particular way.

I consider this moment:
untamed movement between living
beings—joyful in the quiet,

intertwined in a delicate holy.
They move like this,
we move like this:

unrestrained in our contentment,
rich and wreathed with growth.
This is what I mean to say:

We are the goldenrod against
the blue, we are also
sparrows, released and free:

Every   single   thing   before you is collecting dust.

Radishes at the Grocery

My body stood gray, stood still
in front of the radishes.
November is a curious time for a cloud
of unexpected color.

The collective noun is *bunch*;
shouldn't it be staggering, somehow bigger?
       galaxy, bevy, infinity?
Yes. The infinite of radishes, gathered
with impeccable aimlessness, under hard light
and forced rain sat red, sat damp—
white root antennae reaching.

I stood in a Wednesday morning crowd
touching them—slick root, smooth wet,
fingertips to face—that swift,
startling joy.

Something I Might Say

If you and I sat face to face I might say
I've opened my body to many men—
I don't know what *many* means to you,
but not more than three is what I actually mean.
I might also say: I've run many miles—
these legs and small feet moving quickly—
but *many* here means much more than three.
I might also say that I'm ashamed of that one
night I put salt on night crawlers and with delight,
watched them turn inside out. I might tell you
I run because I'm afraid to look like my mom's side.
I might tell you I'm afraid to not be loved.
I might also say that my only true happiness
is a lake in Tennessee and what does that mean
for the rest of my life? I might be terrified to mention
that sometimes, only sometimes,
when I made my mother upset she made me bleed.
What I might be trying to say is:
I'm not sure how I exist in this space—
in this body—in this air.
Anyway, I might end up completely alone.
Anyway, I might end up complete.

An Early Morning Meditation on Movement

It is February 22nd, the empty rooms of my heart
echo. Today, I'm wearing a denim shirt
and a green scarf, drinking coffee, eyelids heavy

and purple. This morning I woke with a lover—
three years ago, he was married to a mild woman
and I slept with my husband   then—

ghosts now, both of them, though not dead.
Here I place my feet on the ground. Yesterday,
the same. Tomorrow, the same. In 100 years,

still in my denim shirt, the same. I am a small
woman and loneliness is a dead dog decomposing
in July heat, the face of God, a chipped tooth,

an unripe tomato, small bones in my hands
broken, an ill-fitting shirt. But today, loneliness
is a cup of coffee, no sugar and I, a sad woman

with a scarf. This is how we move through life.

The Ex-wife of My Lover Wears a Ponytail to Drop the Kids to School

Two hours before, his mouth on my neck—
we noise in the unharmed-dawn,
take inventory of each other's chests,
spaces we pour into easily:
        the vacant spots,
        rooms with rot and rigor,
        hallways ripe with want.

I press my palm into his sternum,
envision my hand on his bones—
in two hours her slender neck will be exposed
to the air of *this* morning.

I am with her ex-mate, and she is a ghost here:
tell me,
        how does love fail so miraculously?

O Curious God

The sun is blotted out on this side of my world—
which is to say it hasn't stopped snowing for hours.

How can I have the stomach to pine about love and
full moons and bright hot heart break? People are dying;

a sickness washing over our old and sad, dogs and beaten
children are being buried, inches piling on their flattened heads

in this valley of upset. And yet, I can't shake the way
my lover's hands look as he serves me coffee in the mornings,

I lie quiet and bare under his blankets. Or when I wake
in the roundness of the one o'clock hour

because he shakes the bed scratching his ear.
O Perplexing One, is it I who hold the meanness

in my hands that I can write about bodies, naked
and vulnerable, and waffles made by the man I love?

Or is it You who allows such a gray veil?

Pregnancy Litany, in Gratitude

This is a thing they do, the small girl and her mother:
arrive to the fence,
          a temple door to two hooved gods
and offer, in flat palms, a sacrifice.
The small girl and her mother stop to feed two horses on a hill
off a summer highway.

In the space between these four animals exists some fruit, gallons
of warm blood pumping, and a quiet kindness meant for holy
forgiveness.

The beasts have their barn beyond the road,
the mother, a vicious inconsistency, and the small girl only
has her mother.

The two horses concede curve of neck to the small girl's hand
as if to release her guilt
as if to nurture her shyness toward backhand,
as if to sigh *not all big beasts are mean beasts*
          which the small girl, somewhere, understands.

This is a prayer of gratitude.

How to Remember Your Mom

Walk around your apartment—pad softly, a quiet cat in the sun not waking the rabid dog of too-many memories. *Remembering* can sometimes be cruel. Pick up your dishes, place them in the sink. Do not leave your water glass next to your bed. Re-read the books she read to you as a child—take the words and roll them around on your tongue. Conjure the sweetness of a summer day, the way her hair moved with the windows down. She glances over at you, radio up, and smiling. Can you smell the corn ripening? Count the hot-air balloons floating—sometimes there are zero, an empty sky. Sometimes the blue is blotted by sixteen-thousand-five-hundred-and-eighty-two balloons. Keep counting.   Keep counting. Take inventory of the colors disappearing. Summon the shine of her smile—she laughs, a river swift from her mouth. Do not throw heavy stones into the current; instead, lie very still and listen to the hum of her life.

Pregnancy Litany, in the Dark

You who are god of two horses on a hill, you spindle-spine sorrow
thing: see me. You who are many handed and heavy with rod
and gallows, thin-veined and all knowing: consider the siege of
sandhill cranes, consider my migration and forgive. You who are
a collective of heartbreak, the braided being of lonesome and lust:
see, this, the darkest crest of a field and I, walking the rows with
bare feet.

Pregnancy Litany, in Ellipses
after Harryette Mullen

One small woman can only...Keep track of blood in...Turn the lights
on when...Each heartbeat keeps...Replenish your...Let the night lay
heavy on...Put your finger in the...Inspect toilet paper for...Count
the blood clots when...Set your alarm for every...Try not to stand up
too...There will be blood on...and under...Count seconds between
the pain of...Your vagina will be tender; make sure you...It's
acceptable to overreact when...Don't refer to the thing as a...How
much can a girl...Emptying a uterus will only...Of course, people will
ask, but...*Miscarriage* is a hard word to...

The Rooms of My Heart

There is one where I'm standing at the stove pan-frying squash
in early October. There's another one where I'm cradling a small
baby, blonde, whose name is Song-Bird. In one large room there
is an intricate weave of alley-ways where stray cats come to the
sun out of small garages, clean between their claws, tap me, as I
find my way home, with their tails. In another I'm standing in Lake
Huron; my arms draped like muslin on my body, letting the water
lick my legs. There's one tiny room where my pregnancy is viable—
again I walk to this space—flat-palm-press my belly—again and
again. One has twinkle lights on copper wire, stained glass, and
no floors or walls, and is actually not a room at all. Yet another I
am small in a pink swimsuit, my grandmother sits, legs dangled in
the blue pool. There's one where I'm kissing my lover for the first
time—a July afternoon sauntering by the window. In this one I'm
in a gray La-Z-Boy watching *90210*. Next to that one I'm catching
a sunfish with my cousin, its body shimmers in my slight hand.
My dad is still alive, intact. In another, I don't bleed on the clinic
floor in late December and my lover brings yellow flowers to the
hospital, they sit on the window-sill, warm.

Pregnancy Litany, after the Miscarriage

The young artist in her cotton dress says,
      there is death and then life on either side of it.

She does not know the palm-sized blood clot
sliding from between my legs,
or the mad moment of loneliness in every empty room,
or my witness, the mute moon, silver thread of a thing,
or the sickle cat curled at my feet while the bowl
to catch the sacrifice is a toilet.

I say, to correct her,
      there is death and then blood on either side of it,
      under my fingernails, on the rug,
      on empty cupboard handles,
      smeared on my thighs like sunlight
      on a hill where two horses stand,
                  quietly looking.

July

I watch the man and his son check their limb lines
along the shore. The man, barrel chested and sandy

blond, the boy his exact match just smaller and slightly
pale. Even from where I stand, outside the boat and 21

years later, I can feel sorrow leaking outside of the man—
a longing for something that has recently packed up

her bags and her kids and walked out the front door.
The house she left had a porch, a swing, a small white

fence around the garden. The life she left could have
been different. She wanted it to be different. But for now

it isn't and the man and his son troll the early morning lake
searching for channel cats caught up on hook and line.

There is a certain sadness that breaks inside our chests,
but also, also, there is a certain sweetness.

Late Summer Vacation on the Lake

It is September. Six feet from a shale-lined shore
a small-mouth bass swims—dorsal erect, confused
in the water weeds. This is a dying fish and he
has found me on the phone with my lover,
pacing the dry-line. The bass follows closely
as he says, again disappointedly,
> *...but I'm giving you all I can.*

Evening wake knocks the dying fish against
the stones in a hollow named Mirror Cove.
It's so close I see his speckled body, slick in green
Tennessee water. Nine months ago, I miscarried
my lover's baby; he held me in the winter mornings
as I bled. And now, 600 years later, we bark back
and forth about pain into a phone. I watch the bass.
Death follows a cursed woman,   I am convinced.

Litany for the Afraid

Let me take the long road home
     and walk it.
     Walk it while the sun screams
     and sets and burns and lights—
     I'm not afraid of that.
Let me please take inventory of each line
     on his face—
     if the ground opened and I, walking,
     fell in I'd want him to know.
Let me holler from the side window,
     hey you, what's your name
     and she might say Paige or Ashley or Grace.
Let me tell Grace that she is absolutely beautiful
     and she shouldn't be afraid of the sun
     or the man who hit her.
Let me tell him I'm afraid each time he leaves
     that he'll decide differently,
     that he'll want a different body next to his.
Let me yell prayers to the sunrise—
     each soft purple, each bright
     beam something to quell fear.
Let the tulip heads hang heavy
     and please let me tell my mother
     that I'm sorry.
     That I was afraid every time she
     walked in the room,
     but I still love her.
Let each bite of meat remind us—
     we are absolutely animal.
     All wild-run and grass in our legs.
Let me again say:
     I'm sorry
     or
     I absolutely know
     or
     how can I help
     or
     I love you though you've destroyed me.

My Lover and I Fight Again

I am absolutely alone—the only
woman to walk on Neptune,
the watery god of this universe.
He invites me to drown in yesterday's
misery, "Remember when he said he's
never happy?" *He didn't mean me*, I say
to the blue-blood god—*not me*.
I am the only woman to speak
to a god this way. I am not afraid
to drown. I don't hold my breath
but I do hold my lover's words tight
and tender—a life preserver tossed.
I am absolutely alone, walking
on the ocean, salt on my face.
I sit down quietly. What else
is there to do on the water—alone?
Yes, my lover did say he's unhappy
all the time, but does he mean me?
The waves are too high—I can't see
land—but who really is happy?
Who, actually, stands on two legs,
heavy and grounded? *What is stable?*
I ask Neptune. I am not afraid to drown
alone in the chest of a god.

Thirteen Ways of Looking at Punching the Wall

1. Yes, I balled up my small hand
   and, knuckles out, hit the wall
   outside of my bathroom on a Monday.

2. Consider this particular anger
   that propels *this* violence.

3. Those small bones, earlier in the night,
   meticulously moved with both grace
   and habit, opening a bottle of red wine.

4. The length of my fingers had a purple spill—
   a bruise pooling at the base of my bones,
   chunks of skin torn from my hand;
   only trace amounts of blood
   stamped on the wall.

5. I taste this madness, this violence:
   lust for it like the last supper:
   skin and blood and the harmony
   between betrayal and betrayed.

6. I let it bloom from the center
   of my chest—a wild thistle blooming,
   searching for full sun, intense heat.

7. The wall, I tell ya, really had it coming.

8. How beautiful the bruised hand,
   how beautiful the wine bottle,
   how beautiful the stupidity in punching a wall,
   how beautiful the vibration in my body,
       the pain, the stutter and gasp, the complete stop.

9. *Everything stops at hope*, I told a student recently
   while reading Emerson. I mean for it
   to be true in all things.

10. What'd the wall ever do to you,
    my friend asked jokingly.

11. The release of tension: it was a miracle.

12. Six days later I still can not
    open my hand.

13. In the beginning, purple unfurled
    before the good god felt moved to punish the flesh—
    opening under the sun
    brining the delicate daylight.

My Lover Leaves My Bed

He moves through the gray morning; parting the air with his body, leaving *before* behind him. Curtains crease to let in a wet dawn, a fresh summer just beyond us, kept at bay by glass. This is a slow morning, his motion sleek, silence rubbed into the walls, my skin marked with his mouth.

I consider his ex-wife: the one who split herself into three different parts, each one resembling him. Spreading her legs, making him a father.

And I consider who I am—a singular body: two breasts, one ribcage, an empty cup for a uterus. Legs that unfurl, making him divorced.

Two women—just as any women.

New Snow on Rooftops Right before 10 a.m.

He tells me he made a call for a vasectomy,
we're both still sweaty from sex—what can I say to this?
A dumb dove of disbelief caught in my throat
and all I can ask is *why now*?

He doesn't know two nights ago I found a specialist
who might open my lame womb to life.
He doesn't know that the beak of hope has pinched
my skin and I'm still bleeding from it.

He apologizes, *I'm sorry, I don't want more children.*
Do you want a baby? As if it's a math equation to figure:
if *x* is a past miscarriage and *y* is a recent divorce
can you solve for longing?

Yes, I think. Her hair is a silk robe and her
thumbnails are bird seed and her mouth
is a perfect moon and her mother
a small statue erected to forgotten rivers.

It's your body, I say as I nest next to his ribs.
Settle in the movement of breathing—
relaxing into the notion of us—for however long—
just us.

A Poet's History Lesson: a Lecture with Bullet Points

- You will break your elbow in 1st grade after landing, twiggy-arms extended, in the gravel after jumping from an in-flight swing. Drunk with bright guilt, you will hide under the pine trees near the curly slide. You won't remember anything else from that day or the next.

- Aaron, at 16, will kiss your mouth in his S-10, in your barn, in a small gazebo at Wildcat Park while the stars, as young as you in another life, blush when his hand cups your very small breast.

- He punishes you, for whatever reason, by cheating with Lori at church camp.

- After Aaron, *trust* dissolves from your pocket-sized dictionary.

- Once in college, you will be drying your hair and you'll move your neck too quickly; your neck will strain unnaturally. You drive to the E.R. alone.

- In grad school, another poet comments *you sure like to be naked* and you'll say something astoundingly dumb—you kiss his mouth. You're married, he's engaged, your shirt is off.

- 20 years after Lori and Aaron show up at your small town's firework display, you'll find yourself sitting in an upstairs apartment alone. A small lit candle spilling wax.

- Your ex-husband will date a girl you don't like; your current lover has three kids and you can not conceive.   Absolutely there is no truth larger than the one that's stuffed into the pocket of heartache.

The Ex-wife of My Lover Is a Good Mom

He reminds me weekly—
>   *We parent well together*, he'll say,
>   *She's such a great mother.*

As if to exploit that small empty room inside my body;
he walks the perimeter, laying hands on the walls
checking for structural integrity.

As if she has rooted deeply and I am
haphazard ditchside daffodils.

As if I am to conjure up a black and white photo
of a sweet woman standing near a bicycle in slacks.

As if I am the fog that unfurls in his early morning,
confusing his sense of direction.

I nod my head, say
>   *yes. Yes, of course she is. Yes.*

What else is there for me to say on the wild side of the fence?

Life Lessons for an Infant

At the window, I point out November
to my friend's baby, piece by piece.

It's cold, I say. Each leaf a dying kaleidoscope.
All the apples too heavy, thick sugar,

stiff pulp, no waterfall from that tree.
                              [I point to the tree

then the ground.]

Snow soon —
turning skin glass-brittle and cold,

our bodies leaning into the wild, picking
through dormant bushes for a trace of June-

berries or through the neighbor's trash.
I don't tell her

                         crows are omnivorous—
eating the early-dead on the side of the road,

rotten-sapped fruit. I don't tell her we turn
into bare-bone dogs by mid-January.

I don't tell her we die; we starve
under the wolf moon, moaning

in clear silk-light.

She is heavy on my hip; I open
my mouth to release sparrows through

                         the wall.

Catalog of Assumed Movement
after Tomaz Salamun

Erica is a tombstone of a civil war soldier—his leg amputated,
blood pooling on the gurney, floor slippery with his life. The
name of his lover, Martha, on the tip of his tongue as he tastes
stars. Maybe Erica is a slab of shale on a Tennessee shore,
snakes holding tightly to a limb over water. She is her lover's
tongue opening her body with her own pink muscle. Maybe she
is beautiful: green sea glass, washed up on a pebbled beach,
windy as hell. She has been dipped in oil and peppered with dried
flowers—a sweet-dead thing waiting for the dry lips of a broken-
spirited prince. He and his horse are both brown. She is half blood
and bone—by this time next year, she will be the K key on an
antique typewriter. One small spider will run across her body and
die—just flat-ass die due to heart complications. A cat, who is also
Erica, will chew the legs off this wolf spider. Maybe Erica is already
these things in one thousand different dimensions and in this
one, she sits with wine in her mouth and twilight out her window,
twilight in her palm. Let this be a forward propulsion—

A Prayer for My Shit-head Heart

Let my idiot glass heart hold still—
        be still, you wild thing.
Let the damn thing be steady.
Let it hold, tenderly over its elbows
        skinny stems of daisies—
let each petal unfurl under a spring-
        time sun-rise on the drive to work.
Let this dumb, glass heart notice the geese
        on small islands in the thawing river.
Let my little heart notice their fist-
        sized heads tucked-in under
        their wings.
Let my heart work hard.
Let it dig the grave for my dead-dad,
        lay down his spirit, and scatter his body,
        and get that drunk-air out of his memory.
        Do the hard work, heart. Go on! It's time.
Let this little shit-head heart
        pull itself together.
Let my lover's body settle in on itself
        after midnight when I wake up
        to let the cat out the kitchen door.
Let my loud-ass heart quiet its mouth
        long enough for me to lay lips on my lover's
        shoulders as he stirs while I crawl back in bed
        next to his body.
Let my heart stay tangled in this warm, winter nest.
Let this fat heart eat every full moon.
Let that full moon
        burst through all my veins—let
        light warm my skin.
Let the light be plump as I sing alone
        washing my dishes,   alone,
        with my cat between my feet.
Let my wild heart prick its fingers on all the thorns
Let my fingertips callous
        as each hand grabs the vines.

Let this asshole heart prove it,
        absolutely convince me of all of it
        and every moment. And that if I must
        I will—and I will swallow it whole.
                        Amen.

How to Leave a Chicago Pub after a Panic Attack around 11 a.m.

You take your tame body and the tight fist of grief
and you just walk out.
You allow the steel-cold sky to propel you east
toward the lake, full of rusted ship bones
and fish with human teeth.
You take your very breakable body away,
long bones, ligaments, and all the wet blood, unsteady.
Remember, blooms of your ancestors fell from branches,
soaked the air with rotten-sweetness.
You feel death on your tongue meat,
the spot reserved for sugar.
You teach your body to go,
a congress of starlings flaring from tree-tops.

Midwestern Poet's Incomplete Guide to Symbolism

Every bird is a metaphor; in the center of this country, in between
rivers with native names, guilt waves her hand: a beauty-queen
in a hometown parade. A poet is her trauma and her trauma is
probably a man—white and condescending. Possibly her youth
pastor or math teacher. If she mentions *booze*, it's her dad. If
she mentions *fish* or *the late-night fisherman*, it's absence. If she
mentions *Tennessee*, it's freedom. Other images to consider: dead
deer, hips, peonies, morning sunlight (or is that metonymy), the
moon, egrets flying west, sparrows with broken beaks, snakes
wound, accidentally, in hay bales. Mothers, here, like any spot in
the universe carry big bags—let's not go beyond that. Lovers are
bonfires after homecoming games and honestly, in a poem, grief
scores the winning points. How many country roads conjured to
replace time and space?

Each stanza a bluebird, each semicolon a horse, each enjambment
an alley cat infested with fleas,
                    every moment of longing a red-tailed hawk.

On the Moon
for Charles

Nothing floats like they said it would. I am surprised when I throw
the mug against the wall, it shatters, coffee runs down the paint;
they said I wouldn't cry on the moon. My blood tides differently.
Isolation clots and swells inside my veins causing self-pity that can
not be broken—a common side effect they assure me. Wherever I
go, I am exactly a *safe distance* from the sea; there is no sea on the
moon. They had to remove it after countless poets walked right in,
belting about bones turning to shell and the inhumane foreboding
of returning to Earth. The moon doesn't care how my words
sound so I spit them into my hand—raise my fingertips to the vast
empty, a residue routine from praying on Earth—no one is listening
and the dust collects in the pools of my palm.

I will not be coming home.

Gods Ars Poetica

In the beginning there was no America, no tight-
bodied teen-brunette who doodles his boyfriend's
name on his notebook, no Betsy Ross
with pin-pricked fingertips, no Great Lakes Museum
in Toledo, absolutely no Trader Joe's or Miller Lite
or Abercrombie & Fitch. Humans were created
in Rome or born in Paris or emerged right from the Red Sea.
Telephones were only a thing to whisper loneliness,
mouth to ear, and to talk about architecture
and two-act plays. Writing, specifically poetry,
happened by accident. One woman, petite
and desperate, needed to document sex and meat.

She made lines in the sand: It meant sweat and work.
It meant *satisfaire.* It was good.

ABOUT THE POET

ERICA ANDERSON-SENTER lives and writes in Fort Wayne, Indiana. She teaches high school English and creative writing. Her work has appeared in *Tinderbox Poetry Journal*, the once *CrabFat Magazine, Midwestern Gothic, Off the Coast,* and *Dialogist* among others. Her chapbook, *seven days now*, was published by *The Dandelion Review*. Erica hosts free literary events throughout her city to bring poetry to the public. She holds an MFA in Creative Writing through the Writing Seminars at Bennington College in Bennington, Vermont.

ACKNOWLEDGMENTS

Grateful acknowledgment is made to the following publications where these poems, or earlier versions of these poems, first found a home.

Anti-Heroin Chic: "Writing about Birds on the Anniversary of Your Death;" "How to Leave a Chicago Pub after a Panic Attack around 11 a.m."

CrabFat Magazine: "Breaking Up on the Moon;" "Genesis"

Cutleaf: "Midwestern Poet's Incomplete Guide to Symbolism;" "Gods Ars Poetica;" "The Ex-wife of My Lover Is a Good Mom;" "Pregnancy Litany, after the Miscarriage"

Dialogist: "Physics of a Daughter in Survival"

K'In Literary Journal: "Handbook for the Almost Divorced." This poem also borrows a line from Amy Gerstler's poem "Recipe for Resurrection."

Midwestern Gothic: "Autobiography: Summers at My Babysitter's House"

Off the Coast: "Late Summer Vacation on the Lake"

THANKS

Special thanks to EastOver Press for liking these poems enough to bind them together in a real book. This mighty and thoughtful press has all my love.

Big bountiful boxes of thanks to Brett Elizabeth Jenkins, Sarah Miller Freehauf, Sarah Sandman, and Matthew Meriwether for being my first and most honest readers. Thank you for loving me when I am alone in dark waters, for letting me be the creature I am, and for loving my words enough to believe in them.

Many thanks to Desireé Dallagiacomo and all the serious magick of Undercurrent and Throughline.

A ridiculous amount of thankfulness is stretched out to the men who let me love them and who loved me back.

For these specific residencies, I'm so thankful: Sweet Water Ocean Writing Residency, Sundress Academy for the Arts at Firefly Farms, and Orchard Keeper Writers Residency. So much creation and change happened here.

Baskets full of thanks to Madeline Hennessey and Tessa Gerling. Special thanks to Lake Huron and The Miller House and the ever patient Wilfredo.

More and more thanks to the magic that is Bennington. Specifically, Ed Ochester, Mark Wunderlich, Major Jackson, April Bernard, and my sweet cohort that lived with me at the end of the world every January and June.

Where would I be without the support and love and consistency of Eric Ehlers, Heather and Aaron Senter, Bryce Wiseman, Jeff Blossom, and Hayley Johnson. Several thousand thanks to each of them.

Special applause to Jessica Danger, April Darcy, Christian Whitney, Jason Beer, Kim Fenoglio, and Steve Henn.

And my undying devotion to Edwin Michele Anderson-Senter, the only living being who has all my love.